CW00820189

To Kr

Our oldest daughter
well we would be
proud if she was

OUR TIMES

Have a very Happy
married life

love

Dad xxx
(Kathy)

# OUR TIMES

ROGER MUMBY-CROFT

Matador
9 Priory Business Park,
Wistow Road, Kibworth Beauchamp,
Leicestershire. LE8 0RX
Tel: (+44) 116 279 2299
Fax: (+44) 116 279 2277
Email: books@troubador.co.uk
Web: www.troubador.co.uk/matador

ISBN 978 1784623 180

British Library Cataloguing in Publication Data.
A catalogue record for this book is available from the British Library.

Printed and bound in the UK by TJ International, Padstow, Cornwall
Typeset in 11pt Aldine401 BTRoman by Troubador Publishing Ltd, Leicester, UK

**Matador** is an imprint of Troubador Publishing Ltd

*This book is dedicated to my uncle, Jack Jones,*
*who first aroused my interst in poetry.*

*Also to my wife Kathy and children Ben, Sally and Rebecca*
*without whose support the bottom drawer would have remained full.*

# CONTENTS

# BAD PROGRESSION

We sit under the old shadow of adolescent principle,
    aware of decrying tones, hoping for lost meaning.
Moving to original time, swinging tones of music are
    affecting my mind, thus shielding my open eyes.
From the base religious rise as secular reason falters fails,
    comes the growth of hardness the cry of strident
    political bells.
Lack of trust, a political legacy Elephant and a feel of
    sleaze the lure of self-interest.
Rumbling under the surface. Every old echo and thought
    curses my looking back.
For the voice of my boyhood is feint – no lost.

# RURAL ENVIRONMENT

The evening sky is winter torn, western winds leave the
trees forlorn.
We realise the smells of autumn gold, as the cattle shuffle
in the snow,
   sheep perceived by tinkling bells.
As gently they are shepherded to the fold, are these the
seasons we love to behold, but who guards this rural
idyll.
Who claims to protect the country life, often those who
exploit it most, mad cow disease, foot and mouth.
   Toxic rubbish not collected.
Creating deserts by size, where the only crop is profit.
The land lies barren and bare from over use of pesticides.
No idyll but poisoned land with dust filled skies.

# FLYING TO ITALY

Jagged mile after jagged mile of snow tipped peaks that
  slip beneath the pitted silver wings. The sky to the
  horizon is clear and blue, then I watch a snow storm
  hurrying in.
The steward offers me a coffee with a smile as we float
  above this scene with serene ease reading a paper,
  enjoying the trip.
Five hundred knots yet it seems so slow.
We will arrive within the hour.
How exhilarating flying can be when you can look out at
  the earth on show.

# CHELSEA JANUARY 07

The staccato drumming of rain on the café window.
Wind swirling, curling paper through the air as people
    bent and blown,
        struggle past the picture window that is like a cinema
        screen showing London in all its depth as if it lives
        like an old film on a modern movie.
Taxis, buses, shops and cafés sitting amongst Georgian
    architecture that makes Chelsea seem as though the
    Regency lives in front and not behind the present,
Twenty-first/eighteenth centuries merged in an engaging
    structure of elegant technology.

# EARTH WARNING

The music of Ghia is at work. But is unheard by us.
Gradually our noise will drown that music
We will then no longer be around.

## LOVE

Love is like a circle that constantly moves.
In keeping with the uncertainty of eternity.

# FAMILY CHRISTMAS

The different sheaves of their childhood are stacked in the
 corners of their rooms.
Christmas comes around as they journey from childhood
 to adulthood.
Rooms have a constant presence but we are subject to
 constant change.
Christmas past and present merge into a kaleidoscope of
 memory.
In which lies the family essence like images from a
 fairground ride.

# COAST LIFE

I must return from whence I came to the sea,
    and the sand and the sailing rain.
Where an iron grey sky hangs over an iron grey sea,
    and my thoughts are alive with memories of she.
We walked along this desolate beach where driftwood
    abounds,
Where old shells are ground by the sea to new white sand.
The sound of the gulls and the distant roar of the sea
    seems to bring you close to me,
    you are of the sea, alive and free,
    so I must return from whence I came.

# PORT MEADOW

Estuary-like with wind and gulls,
Port Meadow sits in breezy light.
The wapping of a shackle in the wind;
The mould-green, neglected hulls of cruisers, yachts and
    narrow boats;
Pontoons reaching into the muddy dock;
Collected rubbish seems a blight but has a curiously
    domestic feel.
From this inland sea stretches out a non-English plain
    Serengeti by the Isis stretching to the horizon, filled
    not by African herds of wildebeest, zebras, antelopes
    but English herds of cows, ponies, horses.
Port Meadow is Oxford's lung as walkers, cyclists,
    runners exercise on its green vastness, whilst in winter
    it allows ice-skating to reign.
Those who witness the changing meadow are mesmerized
    by the sight of its unploughed presence.

# S.W. SWEDEN

Sails like toothpicks stand out in the sea.
Blue and yellow flags billow and blow,
As South-West Sweden is on show,
Blue-green sea, pink-white granite,
Houses clinging to island outcrops, painted ochre red,
Where sounds from voices drift over the waves;
As islands and inlets glisten and gleam.
And sails like toothpicks stand out in the sea,
South-West Sweden is on show.

# THE RIDGEWAY

Golden shadows are cast by walking feet
Over the Ridgeway's drover's miles,
Over the wide horizon's curve
Down to the river's greening curl;
What chance to walk with you my love or the
    summer's shining smile.

# STATIONARY

Sat in the traffic jam,
I look to my left
At a small plot of old rural England
Left amongst the maze
Of slip roads, gravel beds
And concrete shards alongside the motorway.
As through binoculars in homage to Grantchester
Opens a small tunnel of green gloom and sleep.
Where an old style is seen
Mysteriously beneath unkempt elders
And hawthorn trees,
Untrod for years, isolated
Unreachable now by foot
No travel on its long-lost pathway.
The remains of the old fence left to gently rot.
There is a beauty to the uncut, tall grass and wild rose
That entwine this oasis.
One's gaze is drawn to a distant view
Just visible through the hedge;
A far more pleasant view than the road ahead.
As the traffic moves on, the plot is lost
Left in tranquillity to moulder,
As the rest of that older England expires.

# A MARCH HOLIDAY

Cornwall lies to the west,
Shrouded as ever by rain and mist.
What older culture lives
Behind the modern tourist face?
Pretty villages nestling by the sea.
Cold moonscapes scar the landscape.
Thank goodness we came by train.
The M5 blocked by a lorry on its side.
We glimpse an ancient Britain on the way to St Austell,
Then via bus to Tregony and Portscatho.
A coastal journey on par with any
As we head to the Plume of Feathers for beer and food,
Then down to the harbour
To catch the evening tide,
Before finding our house;
Put on the lights, we have arrived.

# OXON WATER MEADOWS

With a silent quickening rush
Our water meadows came
As under the Rainbow bridge
The poetic Cherwell gleamed
Sparkling in the evening sun
Rushing as the air creaks.
The kingfisher flashes down
The river to the greening dell
Of small, lush, beflowered meadows
Pockets of vital urban green
Beckon us back to an older scene.
Meadows the norm
Before an industrial storm
Blew away the patchwork quilt of fields
That now only in Oxon is seen.
Encompassed by a wide town
The meadows are like a warning bell
Of danger still to come.

# RIVER CRUISER

I lay within the dark side
Of a brooding autumnal day
Where, as with decaying summer
The boat lies in need of love
To cover its beauty a constant battle
The wind as enemy or at play
Brings violent gusts stripping away
The narrow shelter that lay between.
Notions of safety and despair.
Will we stay afloat another year?
The boat that floats my ideas
May slip beneath the surface.
Mounting problems blowing in on
Both the wind and melancholy.

# DIMENSIONS OF LIFE

Life is a many-folded cloth
Where we wrap our dreams.
Some folds are for daily life
Where we are as we are seen.
Some folds are where we hold our dreams.
Yet there are some special folds
In which we have another reality
Another life in tune with our being
This is where we can love and live
Enjoy life but not as we are told
But to protect this space we must ensure
That the special folds do not unfurl
And leave us in a place we could not endure.

# AN OXFORD EVENING

A Christmas evening at the corner of Saville Road.
Mist enveloping the municipal lamp,
The evening air colden and damp.

Shadows of false Gothic loom from out of the fog.
A college standing over a Victorian Oxford that feels
A presence in the gloom.

Aided by a hint of coal
Smoke kept down by the damp air
You almost see Victorians
Walking there.

The noise of a car starting
Booms through the mist
As if to prove
Modern Oxford does exist.

We turn and wander down
Hollywell Street through the
Town and down Woodstock Road
On our long walk home.

# KATHRYN

My Myfanwy of Summertown
Striding along strong and brown
Taking our children by the hand
Down to the local swimming pool
Do not play the fool you say
The start of another busy day
I loved you then and I love you now

# NORTHERN SKY

The sun shines in the northern sky.
Why is that light so pure,
When looked at in the early evening.
Golden and pale it cascades down
To bathe us in its heat
Making parting so difficult to endure.

# AN EVENING DRIVE IN
OXFORDSHIRE

Between high hedgerows
In the still evening air
Of an Oxon evening
We smell the lilac as
It mingles with the
Pungent scent of linseed
Growing in nearby fields.

Meandering through the country roads.
Radio Three plays Elgar and we talk of many things as
    you drive the car to a country pub.

We sit, bathed in late evening light; the scent of
    jasmine now filling the air.
We finish our Sancerre,
Ready to return to urban blight.

# FREE SPACE

Lose yourself in the surface
Stare straight into its depth
Look at its texture and colour
Watch the reflections of light
Make it appear as you choose.

Space is in its white interior
You are drawn into a vast arena
A passageway into a magical place
Where you can be who you wish
Not be seen for who you are.

You must be quick to
Delve into the structure.

You are staring at a wall
In the Tate Britain soon
They will come and hang
An important picture.

# ALLOTMENT SPACE

A plot of land lies between river and rail
Hemmed by a cascade of new houses that close its vistas
But increase in a strange way its sense of rural space
Entry is by a security gate that hides this urban paradise
Once through, you enter a different place, no sense of
    rush here
No real modernity lest hanging CDs twinkling in the sun
    count as such
Pleasure as much made by the mind as by the spade
A new persona drops like a mantle on your shoulder
All turn into allotmentees, spirit lifted by the tranquillity
Huts, bins and compost heaps, a plethora of neglected
    artefacts
Cold frames made from bricks, glass and plastic
    protecting plants
Hollyhock, Delphinium and Nasturtium add colour, give
    dimension
Fruit trees – apple, pear, plum give height and add perspective
Individual plots mimic the eccentricity of their allotmentees.
Summer evening finds the sun lying low over the meadow
Gathering in the ripening harvest brings almost primeval joy
Soon it will be time to close most of the land down until
    next year.

# LAKE FELLS

The sun setting on the western edge of the fell,
Makes a pattern that speaks of love,
Reaching those enlightened heights of which few can tell.

# HOPE OF SPRING

A splash of red against the silvery morn.
Flowers drowning in the watery sun.
As the frost crystals are borne away in warming rays.
Cock Robin cuts a dash as he hops amongst the stiffened
    shrubs.
Bringing that confidence of spring by keeping the fading
    winter at bay.

# THE THAMES PATHWAY

The Thames path in October is a joy to walk.
Autumn whispers the leaves to the ground.
All you can hear is the gurgling sound of the river
As it flows so swiftly down to the weir.
The evening light is fading as the wind begins to blow
Sending ripples down the stream
Causing eddies to swirl and grow.
The lone pub sits by the Thames
Full of excited anglers
They have caught roach, bream, pike and barbel,
As they swam, unseen, wandering in a ceaseless
    daydream.
The willows create the bank of the river
Curling slowly, meandering through the water meadows
Wither it goes, plushy reed beds under autumn skies
Fields full of winter cabbages are seen close by.
The hedgerow and the river are as one
Both looking cold, brown and slowly turning.
Hip, elder and sloe brighten the day
With flashes of red, black and Prussian blue.
Ubiquitous nettles greening abundantly (verdant)
Await the walker as the path opens up for you.
Take it to that riverside pub
Settle down, enjoy a drink
The next walk will not be
Until the coming of spring.

# ILLUSION

Dozing in my car
By a country high road
Gazing at the rural beauty
That is set out before me.
I see in the distance
A tall, white tower gleaming
Sparkling in the late sunshine.
Where can that tower be?
Why does it gleam so bright?
Then I realise the tricks
That tired eyes can play.
It is a fragment of white feather
Shimmering in the hedgerow
My eyes slowly close
The thought of a feather tower
Lulls me finally to sleep.

# A VIEW FROM PRIMROSE HILL

High on Primrose Hill,
I feel refreshed, alive.
A watery sun shines over the towers of the city.
The wind brings a cool embrace.
A green and measured place
Where the Aviary is set
Against the moving, distant eye.
A hive of physical activity
Joggers, walkers, children playing.
Alive with trees and birds.
How splendid the city
Laid out far below.
From Camden over to Bow
A lofty calm against the energy below.

# FALSE REMEMBRANCE

Why do we celebrate death as an honour?
Why is that more important than vibrant life taken at the
    flood?
War at times may be needed, but is such a human failure.
What good comes from so much wasted blood.
We glorify the idea of war,
Not learn the lessons of prevention or the purpose of
    negotiation;
Nor realise that discussions should be heeded.
So is it better for some to die in mud
In order to satisfy notions of honour in blood?

# DEEP IN OXFORDSHIRE

Deep within the Oxfordshire countryside the sun filters
     through an old sign to Brill.
Elder flowers in profusion; their white flowers nearly
     done.
The remote crossroad with its old oak standing as sentinel
     to continuity.
A gnarled tower by the five bar gate is flanked by hip and
     hoar, acting as a door to a different, managed
     countryside
     where row upon row of barley and wheat grown to order
     for beer and bread stand robustly in the evening air.
Green trees flank the fields, tall grasses weave in the sun,
     sheltering tiny voles and bigger Muntjac deer.
The quiet black tarmac glistens in the sun. Observe tyre
     track patterns in the melting surface like an urban
     footprint impressed upon the remote Oxon
     countryside.

## BECKY

Riding through Summertown on her wartime special
She sits in high delight with happy smile
Shakespeare and champagne, ideology and geography
A-levels passed with a certain style and that happy smile.

# SOUTHWOLD BEACH

Water slipping over shells
Gurgling sand is refreshed
Golden sun drifts away
Sea and moon a merry band
As night comes on by
Tripping by the shore
Ethereal beauty of the sea
As if with tinkling bells
White horses are falling in the moonlight
As we walk along the Southwold shore.

# GATHERING AUTUMN

Green drips ever faster from the trees
Colour slips quietly away as flowers fade
Early morning dampness slips into my life
As the darkness creeps slowly into my day
High summer sounds and smells have drifted
    away
As a new grey becomes the order of the day

# WINTER EMOTIONS

Winter has entwined the mind
All feelings cold and numb
Every thought frozen in time
Emotions feel the chilling wind
That blows in ahead of bold cold fronts
Freezing love into forms of anger and hate
Psychological cold dampens the heat of longing
Forcing us to crack and break into sharpened shards
That destroy new love which from summer springs.

# THE RUNNER
## (BEN)

He ran, it seems as if to catch the very horizon
He felt worry drain away as he ran along the life-filled
    canal
Time was an invention, as he bounded on he felt
    reborn.
His mind cleared as the mist after dawn
He was happy and free
He loved and was loved
His circle drawn.

## HEAD AND MIND

Sometimes I only exist inside my head.
The thought of getting up fills me with dread.

# RITE OF SPRING

Suddenly the feeling comes and the heart is alive again
The pulse is quickened with buds of happiness
A heart lay dormant and numb
For the world in a rare way
Had wrapped it in cold splendour
Then the spring of concord came
Winter's hold, bleak and dark
Was broken as birds sang
You put warmth into my world
And took my frozen life off hold

# RELIGIOUS  WAR

In the year of 2004
Religious war comes knocking at the door.
Certainty of right created extremity of wrong
By groups of militant factions;
Christian, Muslim, Hindu and Jew
All are sure of their spiritual light.
The only god is the one they site
Reason now is growing dim
As fanaticism demands its law.

# THE OLD SPORTS GROUND

I lean upon the rusting gate as bindweed entrails wither in
　　the frost.
The once pristine privet hedge looks shrunken, bare,
　　wind tossed.
A company name echoed in the gate
The letters faded, carelessly bent.
The urban sprawl beyond occupies the company ground
　　where sport once reigned.
The users felt part of a whole,
Playing cricket, football and bowls for the company name
　　in all the leagues.
Now, garages occupy the crease and houses team up on
　　the soccer field.
The bowling green once so proud is now lined with rows
　　of plastic wheelie bins.
A sub-station stands where changing rooms once stood.
All sense of identity gone.
No more big baths, with frozen players hunting the soap.
No mellow music in the club;
No chatter about games just played.
Just neo-modern homes with faded fencing and plastic
　　windows.
There is no society, only individualism, we are told and
　　this echoes in the loss of a collective ethos of old.
The gate, a gently rusting pulse, the estate beyond hard
　　and cold.

## MADRID 2007

Madrid, Madrid how far you seem. Wind blowing down
from the high sierra brought a dull blast to the warm
streets as if people shuddered at a collective memory,
warmth though returns as the wind drops away.
Modern Spain is again on view today. Vibrant, colourful,
full of music, dance, cafés. The essence of Spain is
strong as it was "As I walked out one midsummer
morning". Magnified by a vibrant democracy, what
would Laurie see in this change if he was perchance to
see it again.

# AUTUMN

Golden morning light, cold air dancing
    through my dreams
Autumn arrives playing on my brain
Why does this season excite me so?
The foggy morn comes laden with dampen air, blurring
    sight
Why am I so excited by the thought of what might lie
    beyond my gaze
Why, because the fog forms an existential haze

DEPARTURE

To leave, to part, to go into the enveloping world, be made invisible to each other by the sheer mindlessness of an individual diaspora, passing into the gathered throng, never able to find one's love again.

# OUR TIME

Worry not about certainty;
Fear not the thought
That we will be gone
One day at some date;
That our conscious time
Will ebb and cease;
That what remains will fade,
Merge into the earth's dust.
Rather make the best of the day
"Carpe Diem"
Fill it with purpose
Generate an air of activity
Worry not about certainty.

## THE EVENING GARDEN

The smouldering rays of the sun leap across the late
    evening air, as flowers before the heat will run.
Scented smells bounce off the garden wall as you, my
    love, sit with book and tea, serene amongst the
    garden's bays.

# VISITING THE DOCTOR

The sun's rays light upon the cancer poster.
Rays of warmth illuminate the waiting room.
Sitting in silence, we wait to be seen.
Some ready, some gaunt, some seemingly bright
Where is the 4.40pm appointment?
It will play havoc with the roster.
Action for Life, Post-Natal Monday, Art for Toddlers
Shout from the wall at us.
Please help your doctor to help you
Have an injection against the flu.
Health on an industrial scale
Puts well-being beyond the pale
Are we sure of what's for sale?

# BOTSWANA

How addictive is the subject that is Africa
Your world changes your senses reel
As the sights and sounds break upon your sensitised mind
The warmth, the smell, the normality of the wild life with
    large animals ever present
Make for an entirely different feel to anything within your
    working memory

A bushman in the Kalahari rouses the ancient brain.
As if you strain to remember the Bushman's knowledge
As the interaction stirs long-lost information
You realise what we have lost

The wide blue sky and warming air combine with endless
    bush to create a world of concealed beauty where
    sounds rather than shapes affect your reaction to
    Nature's world
One visit and you are addicted to the substance that is
    Africa

# SKYE GIRL

Long ago I walked the Cuillen Hills along the western
    ridge one long summer eve with honey light reflecting
    on the rusty slopes
Now a lifetime later I remember a glass of Taliskay in a
    Portree Inn, the water of the minches, the colour of
    the fishing boats
Your golden hair embarking on a walk across the island to
    Sligahan and beyond as time stood still but moved
    quickly, oh what became of you Skye girl in the
    unfolding forty years of life, what did you do, go back
    and enjoy a life of hills, heath and the craic

## MOTHERS
## (FOR GRAEME)

From the day we were born, you gave us love
You gave us courage to be who we are

So lucky we were to have a mother such as you
Thank you for your kindness and for everything you did

Thank you for the happiness you gave us every day
Not often enough did we tell you how much you meant
    to us

We will miss the values of Trust, Honesty and Love
You taught us all to know

But more than this we will simply miss you

# CHRISTMAS MARKET

Christmas Eve morning dawns misty and cold
People hurry to the covered market to collect their fare
Little traffic and a ringing bell, evokes an older Oxford
    with echoes of England from Chaucer to Auden

The market appears bold in the dark sitting amongst
    colleagues, shuttered and closed it offers a sense of
    season
Smells of old, come rushing toward you, poultry and meat
    hang from the rafters, fish sparkling from the sea,
    fresh fruit stacked high, vegetables laid out for all to
    see

You enter a world of ancient and modern. The stalls look
    ancient but the traders modern with mobiles at their
    ears as they buy and sell.

The atmosphere with Xmas trees on high and geese
    hanging down evokes that mixture of epiphany and
    pagen which Oxford has always chosen
Gather all your Christmas fare and head back into the
    cold morning light, hoping there is not a traffic
    warden in sight

# INTERVIEW DAY

I am taking my daughter Sally for an interview
Fine Art is the route she wants to take
Is everything ready she asks at 7.30am for a 2.30 date
Hang on I need to plot the route

Do you do nothing properly she shouts, steady I reply
The venue is reached with an air of dynamic calm
A new university building looms through the misty
    afternoon

Park the car and off she goes following directions to the
    interview room
I hang around, go for a coffee, will she do well as she
    seemed in a mood

Two hours pass and back she comes, looking relaxed
Thank you Daddy with a hug and a smile

I melt and will of course do it again in a while

## ANDERS HELSING

Do not stop sailing
Do not forget to hike
Do not stop skiing
Rather remember

My hand on the sail
My feet on the hills
My eyes on the slopes

Remember me with happiness
I loved the sun, the wind and the rain

Remember me with happiness
But not with a numbing pain

## ATTRACTION 1982

My pulse quickens at first sight of you
My heart pumps faster as you approach
My brain commands my eyes to look at you
This tells me you are special, my mind is absorbed by
    an aura of beauty
It sends a message to my physical being
Now it must play its part in winning you

# POVERTY

Dying for want of water
Dying for want of drugs
A man in Africa lost his daughter
A woman in Brazil became ill she died
Both were poor, it is a different law

# ST JOHNS SQUARE

The flags flutter over St Johns Square
Cafés abound in this ancient part of London town
Architecture a perfect mix ancient, modern, Georgian,
    Victorian
The sun's drowning light warms the early morning rush

We sit and listen to the traffic hum as the square fills with
    young busy people
Today is my birthday suddenly I feel as old as the square
However sitting in the open square with croissants, butter
    and coffee eases my frown

I look at St John's tower and a distant steeple, echoes of an
    older age fill my mind
But this is September 4th 2013 to sit with Kathy and our
    girls is a pure delight
Amidst a very modern London scene.

# NETWORKS

Light glancing through a carriage window. A green
    glistening old railway cutting
Aging infrastructure with weeds and assorted rubbish
Bright new train bustling onward out of sight

Computers toiling, mobile phones ringing, business
    on the move using ancient lines in modern times
Hurrying to destinations far and wide, sitting in
    carriages, engaging their brains
Modern commuters, communicating on a global scale

Railways and Internet, the networks that created and
    sustain our world go hand in hand
Until the power runs out

## T I M E ?

What is the relativity of time?
How can we understand?
Theoretical time or even life-time
We are born, we die, a curve or a line
Who knows?
However I want to add value in my-time

# PLAY UP & PLAY THE GAME

I walk stiffly off the court
The pain is gnawing at my leg
My ankles swell and knees creak
Is age like a tendril reaching
Up to take my mobility
So to leave me in need of care?

I will not yet leave the stage
Take the pills, strap-up & play
Is there nobility in carrying on
Maybe not but I will endeavour
To prolong the day my racket
Has its way

# BABY BOOMERS

Please note we are not old
Therefore do not expect us
To do as we are told

Old age is not a condition, it is
A point in the relativity of a
Life-time where all comes together

Do not denigrate old age rather
Ensure it liberates us to practice sedition

What nonsense to see us as our forebears were
When life was so hard it made them old
When they were still young
Never mistake the quality of life
With its longevity
Rather ensure the two come together

Then we can contribute without
Anxiety to the creation of a better society

We will continue to rage against this view of age
We will pursue the continuance of the light
We will not go gently into the night

# A WOODLAND POEM
## WYTHAM

*January*
Snow like a mantle lies
over the high green crown
Blurring all the shapes and hues
Through the tracks and rides
Glistening white untrodden carpet
Covering all that is darkly brown
As Whytham Woods mounts
Its winter show

*February*
Slowly winter is passing by
Ice shards as so many jewels
Amidst cold translucent mud
Snow drops amidst sodden brackens
Pale against the deep hinterland
That protects the hidden crown
The badger set looks cold and bare
As the bold robin struts across a broken
Bough on guard against winter's excess

*March*

Strong March winds bend the wood
Clouds scurry high above the crown
Fallen trees matted in greening moss
Gently rotting away in silent peace
A micro world of teeming insect life
Ensures there is no loss to forest life
Their nutrients enriching the ubiquitous bluebells

This is the month when dell and dale
Are loud with silent ceaseless growth
As crows swirl and cry on high
Seemingly breaking those March winds down

*April*

The misty blue haze of bluebells
Stretches through the greening wood
Like a swelling sea into which
The tall trees can fall and drown

Beyond our gaze the bleat of new born lambs
Is carried on the cold April wind
Deer hide amongst the glens as the
Sent of spring is airborne whilst visitors watch the
    change
Of colours begin

*May*

Slipping down the woodland rides vestiges of a blue
     haze fades
As red campion take their place
Though fewer in number and strength
They are dotted amongst the verdant nettles
On this beautiful May morning
Blue skies highlight the ancient oaks
That rise from the fields of yellow buttercups

It is wild flowers' time to take the woodland stage

*June*

The high verdant crown tops the wood of curling
     green
Thickets of leaves are dappled by the last setting rays
     of the sun
Red campion lonely amongst the ferns gives colour to
     their shades of green that run down the coppiced
     hill
The wood stacks form symmetrical lines as unkempt
     about their base grows an unofficial honeysuckle
     rose.

*July*

Like a long parched tongue the sun withered hill
  reaches towards the woodland crown. Dry
  waterless grass bereft of its sheep beckons you into
  the cool darkened wood, passing into an oasis of
  dappled green the breeze blows warm and deep as
  shots are heard from the glen, unsung the deer die
  in the annual cull.

*August*

The wood looks high against the sky.
When viewed from across the flatness of Port Meadow
The crown stands out on this blustery blue August
  day
As the Thames winds itself to Eynsham it meets
with the lower wood as it comes down to greet
the river in an inspiring meeting of nature.

The cool still green of the wood and the softly flowing
  greening water

*September*

Autumn slides in over summer's heat
Late September sun warms the rides and glen
But cool air now pervades the even tide
Morning mists rise over the wood's resplendent
    crown

A stir is caused by the warming of the day
As if the wood wants the last of summer colour
Before the Autumn gold leads to winter's brown
A pool of light highlights a man-made den where
    children play and animals hide
A throng of walkers fill the still green wood
Humans wanting the last of summer's feel
Walking through the ancient oaks a glorious view
    across the valley appears but on the horizon dark
    clouds can be seen
Soon summer will have been as the cycle of the year
    turns its wheel

*October*

The dusky gloom of an autumnal afternoon
Shows the ancient oaks spreading their boughs like
    woodland sentinels
A carpet of leaves heralds the coming of winter as the
    sweet smell of damp decay pervades the air
Industrial trees are cleaned to make room for natural
    growth as the wood moves both forward and
    backward in time
Nature allowed its way will ensure the wood is well

*November*

The light is rapidly fading spreading down from the
    darkening crown
To all the lanes and rides through the wood
Smoke rises from the chalet that Hans Andersen like
    sits in a clearing
A pale light illuminating the badger set. Stare into the
    gloom and by chance you glimpse a stag hiding in
    a thinning copse.
Then a flight of birds hurrying to roost before the
    darkness completes its evening task.
The fox bides his time before going abroad
As night settles anxious animals perform a survival
    dance


*December*

The low hum of conversation comes seeping through
    the trees, the wood is full of walkers today
All types, walking and talking their way through the
    rides tracks and glens on this mild December
    morn
Golden sunshine dropping from a clear blue sky
    bathes the crown and plays upon fallen trees
    encased in soft green moss like a spotlight on
    actors in a pagan show
However, the end of the year is close, a colder new
    one is peeping through